Financial Fitness:
Simple Strategies for Building Wealth and Financial Freedom

Isaiah E. Derek

All rights reserved. No part of this publication may be reproduced, distributed, or transmitted in any form or by any means, including photocopying, recording, or other electronic or mechanical methods, without the prior written permission of the publisher, except in the case of brief quotations embodied in critical reviews and certain other noncommercial uses permitted by copyright law.

Copyright © Isaiah E. Derek, 2024.

TABLE OF CONTENTS

INTRODUCTION
CHAPTER 1: WHAT IS FINANCIAL FITNESS?
Financial Fitness Definition
Importance Of Financial Fitness

CHAPTER 2: UNDERSTANDING YOUR FINANCIAL HEALTH
Assessing Your Current Financial Situation
Setting Financial Goals
Identifying Areas For Improvement
Seeking Professional Guidance

CHAPTER 3: BUDGETING BASICS
Understanding The Importance Of Budgeting
Steps To Creating A Budget
Tips For Budgeting Success

CHAPTER 4: DEBT MANAGEMENT
Different Types Of Debt
Developing A Plan To Pay Off Debt
Understanding The Importance Of Debt Management
Strategies For Debt Management

CHAPTER 5: BUILDING AN EMERGENCY FUND
Importance Of Emergency Savings
Establishing And Growing Your Emergency Fund
Tips For Managing Unexpected Expenses

CHAPTER 6: INVESTING FOR THE FUTURE
Introduction To Investing And Investment Vehicles
Setting Investment Goals And Risk Tolerance

CHAPTER 7: RETIREMENT PLANNING
Importance Of Retirement Planning
Types Of Retirement Accounts
Strategies For Maximizing Retirement Savings And Achieving Financial Independence

CHAPTER 8: REAL ESTATE AND PASSIVE INCOME
Exploring Real Estate Investment Opportunities
Generating Passive Income Streams
Tips For Successful Real Estate Investing

CHAPTER 9: PROTECTING YOUR WEALTH
Understanding Insurance Coverage

Estate Planning And Asset Protection Strategies
Importance Of Having A Will And Healthcare Directive

CHAPTER 10: FINANCIAL LITERACY FOR LONG-TERM SUCCESS
Continuous Learning And Staying Informed About Personal Finance
Resources For Improving Financial Literacy
Building A Mindset For Long-term Financial Success

INTRODUCTION

Welcome to "Financial Fitness: Simple Strategies for Building Wealth and Financial Freedom." In this book, you will embark on a journey towards mastering the art of financial well-being and achieving true financial freedom.

In today's fast-paced world, the importance of financial fitness cannot be overstated. Whether you're just starting your financial journey or looking to enhance your current financial situation, this book is designed to provide you with the essential knowledge, tools, and strategies to build wealth, secure your financial future, and ultimately live life on your own terms.

I understand that navigating the world of personal finance can feel overwhelming at times, with complex terminology, conflicting advice, and seemingly endless options to consider. That's why the approach is centered around simplicity and practicality. I believe that achieving financial fitness doesn't have to be complicated or daunting. By focusing on simple yet effective strategies, you can take control of your finances and work towards your financial goals.

In "Financial Fitness," You will cover a wide range of topics, from understanding your current financial health and creating a budget to managing debt, investing for the future, and planning for retirement. You will explore the power of passive income, the role of real estate in wealth-building, and the importance of protecting your assets. Throughout each chapter, you'll find actionable advice, real-life examples, and practical tips to help you apply the concepts to your own financial situation.

Whether your goal is to pay off debt, save for a comfortable retirement, build a nest egg for your children's education, or achieve financial independence, this book will serve as your comprehensive guide to success. By implementing the simple strategies outlined within these pages, you'll be well on your way to financial fitness and freedom.

So, are you ready to take control of your finances, build wealth, and create the life of your dreams? If so, let's dive in and begin your journey towards financial fitness together.

CHAPTER 1: WHAT IS FINANCIAL FITNESS?

Financial Fitness Definition

Financial fitness refers to the state of having strong financial health and well-being. It encompasses various aspects of personal finance, including income, expenses, savings, investments, debt management, and overall financial stability. Someone who is financially fit has a solid understanding of their financial situation, practices responsible money management habits, and is well-prepared to achieve their financial goals.

Importance Of Financial Fitness

1. Financial Security: Being financially fit provides a sense of security and stability, allowing you to weather unexpected expenses, emergencies, or life transitions without undue stress or hardship.

2. Freedom and Flexibility: Financial fitness enables you to have more control over your life and choices. You can pursue opportunities, goals, and experiences that align with your values and aspirations without being constrained by financial limitations.

3. Achievement of Goals: Whether it's buying a home, starting a business, saving for education, or planning for retirement, financial fitness lays the foundation for achieving long-term financial goals and aspirations.

4. Reduced Stress: Financial problems are a significant source of stress for many people. By achieving financial fitness, you can reduce stress levels and improve overall well-being, leading to better mental and physical health.

5. Generational Wealth: Building financial fitness not only benefits you, but also your future generations. By instilling good financial habits and passing down wealth responsibly, families can create a legacy of financial stability and prosperity.

6. Ability to Give Back: Financially fit you have the opportunity to give back to your communities, support causes they care about, and make a positive impact on the world through charitable donations, volunteer work, or other forms of philanthropy.

In essence, financial fitness is not just about having a large bank account or luxurious possessions; it's about achieving financial peace of mind, living within one's means, and making informed decisions that support long-term financial well-being and fulfillment.

CHAPTER 2: UNDERSTANDING YOUR FINANCIAL HEALTH

Understanding your financial health is the first step towards achieving financial fitness and building wealth. It involves assessing various aspects of your financial situation, identifying strengths and weaknesses, and gaining clarity on your overall financial standing. By understanding your financial health, you can make informed decisions, set realistic goals, and develop strategies to improve your financial well-being.

Assessing Your Current Financial Situation

1. Income: Start by evaluating your sources of income, including wages, salaries, bonuses, rental income, investment returns, and any other sources of revenue. Calculate your total monthly and annual income to understand your earning capacity.

2. Expenses: Next, examine your monthly expenses, including fixed expenses (such as rent/mortgage, utilities, insurance premiums) and variable expenses (such as groceries, dining out, entertainment). Track your spending over a period to identify areas where you can cut back or optimize expenses.

3. Assets: Take stock of your assets, including cash savings, investments (such as stocks, bonds, mutual funds), retirement accounts (401(k), IRA), real estate properties, and valuable possessions (vehicles, jewelry, collectibles). Determine the total value of your assets and your liquidity.

4. Liabilities: Evaluate your liabilities, including outstanding debts such as mortgages, car loans, student loans, credit card balances, and any other loans or financial obligations. Calculate your total debt load and assess its impact on your financial health.

Setting Financial Goals

Once you have a clear understanding of your current financial situation, it's essential to set specific, measurable, achievable, relevant, and time-bound (SMART) financial goals. These goals can include:
- Building an emergency fund to cover unexpected expenses.
- Paying off high-interest debt to become debt-free.
- Saving for short-term goals (vacation, home renovation) and long-term goals (retirement, children's education).
- Investing to grow your wealth and achieve financial independence.
- Increasing your income through career advancement, side hustles, or entrepreneurship.

Identifying Areas For Improvement

After assessing your financial health and setting goals, identify areas where you can improve and take action to address them. This may involve:
- Creating a budget to better manage your expenses and prioritize spending.
- Developing a debt repayment plan to pay off debts efficiently and reduce interest payments.
- Increasing your savings rate to build an emergency fund and save for future goals.
- Diversifying your investments to minimize risk and maximize returns.
- Seeking opportunities to increase your income through additional sources or investment in self-development.

Seeking Professional Guidance

If you're unsure about how to assess your financial health or develop a plan for improvement, consider seeking guidance from a financial advisor or planner. A qualified professional can provide personalized advice, strategies, and recommendations tailored to your individual circumstances and goals.

Understanding your financial health is a crucial foundation for achieving financial fitness and building wealth. By assessing your current situation, setting goals, identifying areas for improvement, and seeking guidance when needed, you can take control of your finances and work towards a more secure and prosperous future.

CHAPTER 3: BUDGETING BASICS

Budgeting is the cornerstone of financial management, providing a roadmap for effectively managing your money, controlling expenses, and achieving your financial goals. By creating and adhering to a budget, you gain insight into your income, expenses, and spending patterns, empowering you to make informed financial decisions. In this section, we'll delve into the fundamentals of budgeting and offer practical guidance for creating a budget that works for you.

Understanding The Importance Of Budgeting

1. Financial Awareness: Budgeting allows you to gain a clear understanding of your financial situation by tracking your income and expenses. It helps you identify areas where you may be overspending or where you can potentially save money.

2. Goal Setting: A budget serves as a tool for setting and achieving financial goals. Whether you're saving for a down payment on a house, paying off debt, or planning for retirement, a budget provides a roadmap for reaching your objectives.

3. Expense Control: By creating spending limits for different categories of expenses, a budget helps you control your spending and avoid unnecessary purchases. It enables you to distinguish between needs and wants and prioritize essential expenses.

4. Emergency Preparedness: Budgeting allows you to set aside funds for unexpected expenses or emergencies, such as medical bills, car repairs, or home maintenance. Having an emergency fund provides financial security and peace of mind.

Steps To Creating A Budget

1. Calculate Your Income: Start by determining your total monthly income, including wages, salaries, bonuses, and any other sources of revenue. If your income fluctuates, use an average based on past earnings.

2. List Your Expenses: Make a list of all your monthly expenses, categorizing them as fixed (e.g., rent/mortgage, utilities, insurance) or variable (e.g., groceries, dining out, entertainment). Be thorough and include both essential and discretionary expenses.

3. Set Spending Limits: Allocate a specific amount of money to each expense category based on your income and financial priorities. Aim to cover essential expenses first, such as housing, utilities, and debt payments, before allocating funds to discretionary spending.

4. Track Your Spending: Keep track of your expenses throughout the month to ensure that you're staying within your budgeted amounts. Use a budgeting app, spreadsheet, or pen and paper to record your expenditures and compare them to your budgeted amounts.

5. Adjust as Needed: Periodically review your budget to assess your progress, identify any areas where you may be overspending or underspending, and make adjustments as needed. Flexibility is key to maintaining a successful budget.

Tips For Budgeting Success

1. Start with a realistic budget that reflects your current financial situation and priorities.
2. Be honest with yourself about your spending habits and avoid underestimating expenses.
3. Prioritize essential expenses such as housing, food, and transportation before allocating funds to discretionary spending.

4. Build an emergency fund to cover unexpected expenses and avoid relying on credit cards or loans.
5. Involve your family members or household members in the budgeting process to ensure everyone is on board and committed to the plan.

In conclusion, budgeting is a vital tool for achieving financial stability, reducing financial stress, and working towards your long-term financial goals. By following the budgeting basics outlined above and staying disciplined in your financial habits, you can take control of your finances and pave the way for a brighter financial future.

CHAPTER 4: DEBT MANAGEMENT

Debt management is an essential aspect of personal finance that involves effectively handling and minimizing debt to achieve financial stability and long-term prosperity. Whether it's student loans, credit card debt, or mortgages, understanding how to manage debt responsibly is crucial for maintaining financial health.

Different Types Of Debt

Understanding the different types of debt is crucial for making informed financial decisions and effectively managing one's finances. Debt comes in various forms, each with its own characteristics, terms, and implications. By understanding the distinctions between different types of debt, you can make strategic choices about borrowing and repayment. Below are the common types of debt and their key features:

1. **Good Debt vs. Bad Debt:**
   - Good Debt: Good debt typically refers to loans used to finance assets or investments that have the potential to increase in value over time or generate income. Examples include student loans (investing in education), mortgages (buying a home), and business loans (starting or expanding a business).
   - Bad Debt: Bad debt, on the other hand, is debt incurred for non-essential purchases or depreciating assets, often with high-interest rates and little to no potential for long-term financial gain. Examples include credit card debt used for luxury items, high-interest personal loans for vacations or shopping sprees, or payday loans with exorbitant interest rates.

2. **Secured vs. Unsecured Debt:**
   - Secured Debt: Secured debt is backed by collateral, such as a home or a car, which serves as security for the lender in case the

borrower defaults on the loan. Common examples of secured debt include mortgages and auto loans. Failure to repay secured debt can result in the loss of the collateral.
- Unsecured Debt: Unsecured debt does not require collateral and is based solely on the borrower's creditworthiness. Examples include credit card debt, personal loans, and medical bills. While unsecured debt doesn't put specific assets at risk, lenders may pursue other collection methods, such as legal action or wage garnishment, to recover unpaid debts.

3. Fixed-Rate vs. Variable-Rate Debt:
- Fixed-Rate Debt: With fixed-rate debt, the interest rate remains constant throughout the life of the loan, providing stability and predictability in monthly payments. Mortgages and some personal loans often offer fixed interest rates.
- Variable-Rate Debt: Variable-rate debt, also known as adjustable-rate debt,

features interest rates that can fluctuate over time based on changes in market conditions. While initial rates may be lower than fixed rates, variable-rate debt exposes borrowers to the risk of rising interest costs, potentially leading to higher monthly payments.

4. Installment Loans vs. Revolving Credit:
- Installment Loans: Installment loans involve borrowing a fixed amount of money upfront and repaying it over a set period through regular, fixed payments. Mortgages, auto loans, and student loans are examples of installment loans.
- Revolving Credit: Revolving credit allows borrowers to access a predetermined credit limit and borrow as needed, with the option to repay and reuse the credit line repeatedly. Credit cards and home equity lines of credit (HELOCs) are common forms of revolving credit.

Understanding the nuances of different types of debt empowers you to make informed borrowing decisions, prioritize debt repayment effectively, and ultimately work towards achieving financial stability and freedom. By distinguishing between good and bad debt, evaluating secured versus unsecured debt, considering fixed versus variable interest rates, and understanding installment loans versus revolving credit, borrowers can navigate the complexities of debt management with greater confidence and control.

Developing A Plan To Pay Off Debt

Developing a structured plan to pay off debt is a critical step towards achieving financial freedom and reducing financial stress. By creating a clear roadmap for debt repayment, you can prioritize your debts, allocate resources effectively, and make consistent progress towards becoming debt-free. Below are steps to develop a comprehensive debt repayment plan:

1. List Your Debts: Begin by compiling a detailed list of all your debts, including credit card balances, student loans, auto loans, personal loans, and any other outstanding obligations. Note the outstanding balance, minimum monthly payment, and interest rate for each debt.

2. Organize by Priority: Prioritize your debts based on factors such as interest rates, outstanding balances, and terms. Consider focusing on high-interest debts first to minimize interest costs over time, or opt for the debt snowball method, which prioritizes paying off smaller debts first to gain momentum.

3. Set Clear Goals: Establish specific, measurable goals for debt repayment, such as paying off a certain amount of debt by a certain date or becoming debt-free within a specified timeframe. Having clear objectives provides motivation and direction for your debt repayment efforts.

4. Allocate Resources: Determine how much you can realistically afford to allocate towards debt repayment each month. Review your budget and identify areas where you can cut back on discretionary spending to free up additional funds for debt repayment. Consider reallocating windfalls such as tax refunds or bonuses towards debt reduction.

5. Choose a Repayment Strategy: Select a repayment strategy that aligns with your financial goals and preferences. Common strategies include:
- Debt Snowball: Paying off debts in order from smallest to largest balance, regardless of interest rate, to build momentum and motivation.
- Debt Avalanche: Paying off debts in order from highest to lowest interest rate to minimize interest costs and achieve faster overall debt reduction.
- Consolidation: Consolidating multiple debts into a single loan with a lower interest rate or more favorable terms,

simplifying repayment and potentially reducing monthly payments.

6. Negotiate with Creditors: Reach out to your creditors to explore options for reducing interest rates, waiving fees, or negotiating repayment terms. Many creditors are willing to work with borrowers facing financial hardship to find mutually beneficial solutions.

7. Monitor Progress: Regularly monitor your progress towards debt repayment and adjust your plan as needed. Celebrate milestones along the way, such as paying off a credit card or reaching a specific debt reduction goal, to stay motivated and focused on your financial journey.

8. Stay Committed: Remain committed to your debt repayment plan, even when faced with challenges or setbacks. Remember the long-term benefits of becoming debt-free and stay disciplined in your financial habits to achieve your goals.

Developing a plan to pay off debt requires careful consideration, discipline, and perseverance. By prioritizing debts, setting clear goals, allocating resources effectively, choosing a repayment strategy, negotiating with creditors, monitoring progress, and staying committed to your plan, you can take control of your finances and work towards a debt-free future.

Understanding The Importance Of Debt Management

1. Financial Freedom: By reducing and managing debt, you can free yourself from the burden of monthly payments and high-interest charges. This, in turn, provides greater financial flexibility and enables you to allocate more money towards savings, investments, and other financial goals.

2. Improved Credit Score: Responsible debt management, such as making timely payments and keeping debt levels low, can positively impact credit scores. A higher credit score not only opens up opportunities for favorable interest rates on loans and credit cards but also reflects positively on financial credibility.

3. Reduced Stress: Debt can be a significant source of stress and anxiety for individuals and families. By taking proactive steps to manage debt effectively, such as creating a repayment plan and sticking to a budget, you can alleviate financial strain and improve overall well-being.

4. Financial Goals Achievement: Excessive debt can hinder progress towards achieving financial goals, such as saving for retirement, purchasing a home, or starting a business. By managing debt wisely, you can redirect funds towards your goals and work towards building wealth and financial security.

Strategies For Debt Management

1. Assess Your Debt: Start by compiling a comprehensive list of all your debts, including balances, interest rates, and minimum monthly payments. Understanding the full scope of your debt obligations is the first step towards effective debt management.

2. Create a Budget: Develop a realistic budget that outlines your income and expenses, including debt payments. Allocate a portion of your income towards debt repayment while ensuring you have enough to cover essential expenses and savings goals.

3. Prioritize High-Interest Debt: Focus on paying off high-interest debt first, such as credit card balances, as these often carry the highest interest rates and can quickly accumulate interest charges. Consider using the debt snowball or debt avalanche method to accelerate repayment.

4. Negotiate with Creditors: If you're struggling to make payments, consider reaching out to your creditors to discuss hardship options, such as debt consolidation, loan modification, or repayment plans. Many creditors are willing to work with borrowers to find mutually beneficial solutions.

5. Avoid Taking on New Debt: While paying off existing debt, refrain from taking on new debt whenever possible. Cut back on discretionary spending, use cash or debit for purchases, and resist the temptation to rely on credit cards for additional spending.

6. Seek Professional Help if Needed: If you're overwhelmed by debt or struggling to make progress on your own, consider seeking assistance from a credit counseling agency or financial advisor. These professionals can provide personalized guidance and support to help you regain control of your finances.

Effective debt management is essential for achieving financial stability and building a secure financial future. By understanding the importance of debt management and implementing practical strategies to reduce and manage debt, you can take control of your finances, alleviate financial stress, and work towards achieving your long-term financial goals.

CHAPTER 5: BUILDING AN EMERGENCY FUND

An emergency fund is a crucial financial safety net that provides peace of mind and financial security during unexpected events or emergencies. By setting aside funds for unforeseen expenses, you can avoid resorting to high-interest debt or depleting savings earmarked for other purposes. Building an emergency fund is a foundational step towards achieving financial stability and resilience.

Importance Of Emergency Savings

Emergency savings play a critical role in ensuring financial stability and resilience in the face of unexpected events or emergencies. While it's impossible to predict when unforeseen expenses will arise, having a dedicated fund set aside for emergencies provides peace of mind and safeguards against financial hardship. Here's why emergency savings are essential:

1. Financial Protection:
Emergency savings serve as a financial safety net, providing protection against unexpected expenses such as medical emergencies, car repairs, home repairs, or job loss. Having readily accessible funds available can help you navigate challenging situations without resorting to high-interest debt or depleting savings earmarked for other purposes.

2. Peace of Mind:
Knowing that you have a cushion of emergency savings to fall back on in times of need provides peace of mind and reduces financial stress. It allows you to face unexpected events with confidence, knowing that they have the financial resources to weather the storm.

3. Avoiding Debt:
Without emergency savings, you may be forced to rely on credit cards, personal loans, or other

forms of debt to cover unexpected expenses. This can lead to a cycle of debt accumulation, high-interest charges, and financial strain. By having emergency savings in place, you can avoid falling into debt traps and maintain financial stability.

4. Maintaining Financial Goals:
Unexpected expenses can derail progress towards financial goals such as saving for retirement, purchasing a home, or funding education. Having emergency savings allows you to address unforeseen expenses without derailing long-term financial plans. It ensures that savings earmarked for other goals remain intact and continue to grow over time.

5. Flexibility and Independence:
Emergency savings provide you with financial flexibility and independence, enabling you to make decisions based on your needs and priorities rather than being constrained by financial constraints. Whether it's taking time off work to address a family emergency or pursuing

new opportunities, emergency savings provide the freedom to navigate life's uncertainties without financial worry.

6. Faster Recovery from Setbacks:
With emergency savings in place, you can recover more quickly from unexpected setbacks or emergencies. Rather than facing prolonged financial hardship or struggling to make ends meet, you can address the situation promptly and resume normalcy sooner, minimizing the impact on your overall financial well-being.

7. Protection Against Income Loss:
In the event of job loss or a sudden reduction in income, emergency savings can help bridge the gap until alternative sources of income are secured. It provides a buffer to cover essential expenses such as housing, utilities, and groceries during periods of financial instability.

8. Reduced Reliance on Others:
Having emergency savings reduces the need to rely on friends, family, or external sources for

financial assistance during times of crisis. It allows you to maintain your independence and dignity while facing challenges independently.

Emergency savings is the cornerstone of financial planning, providing protection, peace of mind, and flexibility in the face of unexpected events or emergencies. By prioritizing the establishment and maintenance of emergency savings, you can build financial resilience, avoid debt traps, and achieve greater financial security and well-being.

Establishing And Growing Your Emergency Fund

Establishing and growing an emergency fund is a critical aspect of financial planning that provides a safety net for unexpected expenses or financial emergencies. By setting aside funds specifically designated for emergencies, you can protect yourself from financial hardship and maintain stability during challenging times. Here are essential steps to successfully establish and grow your emergency fund:

1. Set a Savings Goal:
Determine the desired amount for your emergency fund based on your living expenses, financial obligations, and personal circumstances. Aim to save enough to cover three to six months' worth of essential expenses, including housing, utilities, groceries, transportation, and insurance premiums.

2. Start Small and Be Consistent:
Begin by setting achievable savings goals, even if it means starting with a modest amount. Consistency is key to building your emergency fund over time. Commit to making regular contributions, no matter how small, and gradually increase your savings rate as your financial situation allows.

3. Automate Savings:
Automate contributions to your emergency fund by setting up automatic transfers from your

checking account to your designated savings account. Treat your emergency fund as a non-negotiable expense, just like rent or utilities, and prioritize it in your budgeting efforts.

4. Cut Back on Non-Essential Expenses:
Identify areas where you can reduce discretionary spending and reallocate those funds towards your emergency fund. Review your budget and look for opportunities to trim unnecessary expenses such as dining out, entertainment, subscriptions, or impulse purchases.

5. Use Windfalls Wisely:
Redirect unexpected windfalls such as tax refunds, bonuses, or cash gifts towards your emergency fund. Instead of splurging on discretionary purchases, use these funds to bolster your savings and expedite your progress towards your savings goal.

6. Set Milestones and Celebrate Achievements:
Break down your savings goal into smaller milestones and celebrate each milestone you achieve along the way. Whether it's reaching a specific dollar amount or saving for a certain number of months worth of expenses, acknowledging your progress can help keep you motivated and on track.

7. Reevaluate and Adjust as Needed:
Regularly review your savings progress and reassess your savings goal and contributions as needed. Life circumstances and financial priorities may change over time, so be flexible and adjust your savings plan accordingly to stay aligned with your goals.

8. Resist Temptation to Dip Into Your Fund:
Reserve your emergency fund for genuine emergencies only and resist the temptation to dip into it for non-essential expenses. Establish clear criteria for what constitutes an emergency and

stick to it to ensure that your fund remains intact when you need it most.

9. Optimize Your Savings:
Consider maximizing the growth potential of your emergency fund by storing it in a high-yield savings account or a money market account. Look for accounts that offer competitive interest rates and minimal fees to help your savings grow faster over time.

10. Stay Committed and Patient:
Building an emergency fund requires discipline, patience, and perseverance. Stay committed to your savings goal, even during challenging times, and trust in the process. With consistent effort and dedication, you'll gradually build a robust emergency fund that provides financial security and peace of mind.

Tips For Managing Unexpected Expenses

Managing unexpected expenses is a crucial aspect of maintaining financial stability and resilience. While it's impossible to predict every financial challenge that may arise, being prepared and having strategies in place can help you navigate unexpected expenses with greater ease. Here are some practical tips for managing unexpected expenses effectively:

1. Build an Emergency Fund:
Establishing an emergency fund is one of the most effective ways to prepare for unexpected expenses. Aim to save three to six months worth of living expenses in a dedicated savings account to cover unforeseen costs such as medical emergencies, car repairs, or job loss.

2. Prioritize Essentials:
When faced with unexpected expenses, prioritize essential needs such as food, shelter, utilities, and transportation. Focus on covering basic

necessities first before addressing non-essential expenses or discretionary spending.

3. Create a Budget:
Maintain a detailed budget that outlines your income, expenses, and savings goals. Having a clear understanding of your financial situation allows you to allocate funds efficiently and make informed decisions about how to manage unexpected expenses.

4. Cut Discretionary Spending:
Temporarily reduce or eliminate discretionary spending on non-essential items such as dining out, entertainment, or luxury purchases when faced with unexpected expenses. Redirect those funds towards covering essential needs or replenishing your emergency fund.

5. Negotiate Payment Plans:
Reach out to service providers, lenders, or creditors to negotiate payment plans or alternative arrangements if you're unable to pay unexpected expenses in full. Many organizations

are willing to work with you facing financial difficulties to find manageable solutions.

6. Seek Financial Assistance:
Explore available resources for financial assistance, such as community organizations, government programs, or nonprofit agencies, that may offer support or relief for specific types of unexpected expenses, such as medical bills or housing assistance.

7. Use Available Benefits:
Take advantage of any benefits or protections available to you, such as insurance coverage, warranties, or employer-sponsored programs, to help offset the costs of unexpected expenses. Review your insurance policies and understand what types of expenses are covered.

8. Avoid Using High-Interest Debt:
Resist the temptation to rely on high-interest debt, such as credit cards or payday loans, to cover unexpected expenses whenever possible. High-interest debt can exacerbate financial

challenges and lead to long-term debt accumulation.

9. Plan for Future Expenses:
Anticipate and plan for future unexpected expenses by regularly reviewing and updating your budget and emergency fund. Incorporate savings goals for specific types of expenses, such as car repairs or home maintenance, to prepare for potential emergencies.

10. Stay Flexible and Resilient:
Remain adaptable and resilient in the face of unexpected expenses. Understand that financial setbacks are a normal part of life, and focus on finding solutions and moving forward rather than dwelling on challenges.

By following these tips and adopting proactive financial management strategies, you can effectively manage unexpected expenses, maintain financial stability, and build resilience against future financial challenges. Being prepared and having a plan in place can provide peace of mind and empower you to navigate unexpected expenses with confidence and control.

CHAPTER 6: INVESTING FOR THE FUTURE

Investing for the future is a cornerstone of financial planning that enables you to grow your wealth, achieve long-term financial goals, and secure your financial future. Whether saving for retirement, funding education, or building a nest egg, investing provides the opportunity to generate returns on capital over time.

Introduction To Investing And Investment Vehicles

Investing is the process of allocating funds with the expectation of generating returns over time. It involves purchasing assets with the goal of increasing wealth, achieving financial goals, and securing future financial security. While investing carries inherent risks, it also offers the potential for capital appreciation and income generation. Understanding the basics of investing and the various investment vehicles available is essential for you looking to grow your wealth and achieve your financial objectives.

Why Invest?
Investing plays a crucial role in wealth accumulation and financial planning for several reasons:

1. Wealth Growth: Investing provides the opportunity for capital appreciation, allowing you to grow your wealth over time through the power of compounding returns.

2. Financial Goals: Investing helps you achieve specific financial goals, such as retirement planning, funding education, purchasing a home, or starting a business.

3. Inflation Hedge: Investing in assets that outpace inflation helps preserve purchasing power and maintain the value of savings over the long term.

4. Income Generation: Many investment vehicles, such as stocks, bonds, and real estate, offer the potential for regular income in the form of dividends, interest, or rental payments.

Key Investment Vehicles:
1. Stocks: Stocks represent ownership stakes in publicly traded companies. Investing in stocks provides the potential for capital appreciation through increases in share prices and may also offer dividend income.

2. Bonds: Bonds are debt securities issued by governments, municipalities, or corporations. Investors lend money to the issuer in exchange for regular interest payments and the return of the principal amount at maturity.

3. Mutual Funds: Mutual funds pool money from multiple investors to invest in a diversified portfolio of stocks, bonds, or other securities. They offer professional management and diversification benefits to individual investors.

4. Exchange-Traded Funds (ETFs): ETFs are similar to mutual funds but trade on stock exchanges like individual stocks. They offer diversification, liquidity, and lower fees compared to traditional mutual funds.

5. Real Estate: Real estate investments involve purchasing properties with the expectation of generating rental income and/or capital appreciation. Real estate can provide diversification and inflation protection to investment portfolios.

6. Commodities: Commodities such as gold, silver, oil, and agricultural products offer opportunities for investment diversification and inflation hedging. Investors can gain exposure to commodities through commodity futures contracts, ETFs, or direct ownership.

7. Retirement Accounts: Retirement accounts, such as 401(k)s, IRAs, and Roth IRAs, offer tax-advantaged ways to save and invest for retirement. These accounts provide incentives for long-term investing and may offer employer matching contributions.

Investing is a powerful tool for building wealth, achieving financial goals, and securing future financial security. By understanding the basics of investing and the various investment vehicles available, you can make informed decisions, build diversified portfolios, and work towards your financial objectives. While investing involves risks, it also offers the potential for significant rewards over the long term. Starting early, staying disciplined, and seeking professional advice when needed are key to successful investing.

Setting Investment Goals And Risk Tolerance

Setting investment goals and determining your risk tolerance are fundamental steps in developing a personalized investment strategy that aligns with your financial objectives and comfort level with risk. By clearly defining your investment goals and assessing your risk tolerance, you can create a portfolio that balances potential returns with the level of risk you're willing to accept. Here's how to set investment goals and evaluate risk tolerance effectively:

1. Define Your Investment Goals:
- **Short-Term Goals:** Identify short-term financial objectives that you aim to achieve within the next one to three years. Examples may include saving for a vacation, purchasing a car, or building an emergency fund.
- **Medium-Term Goals:** Set medium-term goals that you plan to accomplish within three to seven years. This could involve saving for a down payment on a home, funding a child's education, or starting a business.
- **Long-Term Goals:** Establish long-term goals that extend beyond seven years and

focus on building wealth and achieving financial independence. Common long-term goals include saving for retirement, creating a legacy for future generations, or achieving financial freedom.

2. Consider Your Time Horizon:
Your time horizon, or the length of time you plan to hold your investments, plays a crucial role in determining your investment strategy. Longer time horizons generally allow for more aggressive investment approaches, while shorter time horizons may necessitate a more conservative approach to preserve capital.

3. Assess Your Risk Tolerance:
- **Risk Capacity:** Evaluate your financial situation, including income, expenses, assets, liabilities, and cash flow, to determine your capacity to withstand

investment losses without compromising your financial stability.
- **Risk Preference:** Consider your personal comfort level with risk and volatility when investing. Some individuals may be comfortable with higher levels of risk in pursuit of potentially higher returns, while others may prefer more conservative investments to preserve capital and minimize fluctuations.

4. Determine Your Asset Allocation:
Based on your investment goals and risk tolerance, establish an appropriate asset allocation that balances risk and return. Asset allocation involves dividing your investment portfolio across different asset classes, such as stocks, bonds, cash, and real estate, to achieve diversification and manage risk.

5. Reevaluate and Adjust Regularly:
Periodically review and reassess your investment goals, risk tolerance, and asset allocation as your financial situation and life circumstances evolve.

Adjust your investment strategy accordingly to ensure it remains aligned with your objectives and comfort level with risk.

6. Seek Professional Guidance if Needed:
If you're uncertain about setting investment goals or evaluating your risk tolerance, consider seeking guidance from a qualified financial advisor or investment professional. An advisor can provide personalized advice, recommend suitable investment strategies, and help you navigate complex financial decisions.

Setting investment goals and assessing risk tolerance are essential steps in building a successful investment strategy tailored to your individual needs and preferences. By defining clear investment objectives, considering your time horizon, evaluating risk capacity and preference, determining appropriate asset allocation, and periodically reviewing and adjusting your investment plan, you can create a diversified portfolio that maximizes returns while minimizing risk. Remember that investing involves trade-offs between risk and reward, and finding the right balance is key to achieving your financial goals over the long term.

Simple Investment Strategies For Beginners

Investing can seem daunting for beginners, but with the right approach, it can be accessible and rewarding. Here are some simple investment strategies tailored for beginners:

1. Start with Education:
Before diving into investing, take the time to educate yourself about the basics of investing, including different asset classes, investment vehicles, and risk factors. There are plenty of resources available, such as books, online courses, and educational websites, that can help you build a solid foundation of knowledge.

2. Set Clear Goals:

Define your investment goals and objectives. Determine whether you're investing for short-term needs (e.g., a vacation), medium-term goals (e.g., buying a home), or long-term objectives (e.g., retirement). Having clear goals will guide your investment decisions and help you stay focused.

3. Start Small and Gradual:

Begin with small amounts of money that you're comfortable investing. You don't need a large sum of money to start investing. Consider setting up automatic transfers from your bank account to your investment account to make regular contributions over time.

4. Consider Index Funds or ETFs:

Index funds and exchange-traded funds (ETFs) are ideal for beginners due to their simplicity and diversification benefits. These funds track a specific market index, such as the S&P 500, and offer exposure to a broad range of stocks or bonds. They're a cost-effective way to gain instant diversification without the need for active stock picking.

5. Diversify Your Portfolio:
Diversification is key to managing risk in your investment portfolio. Spread your investments across different asset classes (e.g., stocks, bonds, real estate) and sectors to reduce the impact of market fluctuations on your overall portfolio. Avoid putting all your eggs in one basket.

6. Invest for the Long Term:
Adopt a long-term perspective when investing. Avoid trying to time the market or chasing short-term gains. Instead, focus on building a well-diversified portfolio and staying invested through market ups and downs. Over time, the power of compounding returns can work in your favor.

7. Keep Costs Low:
Be mindful of investment fees and expenses, as they can eat into your returns over time. Look for low-cost investment options, such as index

funds or commission-free ETFs, that offer competitive fees and expenses.

8. Stay Informed and Stay Disciplined:

Stay informed about your investments and the broader financial markets. Monitor your portfolio regularly, but avoid making impulsive decisions based on short-term market fluctuations. Stick to your investment plan and remain disciplined in your approach.

9. Consider Retirement Accounts:

Take advantage of tax-advantaged retirement accounts, such as a 401(k) or IRA, if available. These accounts offer tax benefits and can help you save for retirement while potentially reducing your current tax liability.

10. Seek Professional Guidance if Needed:

If you're unsure about how to start investing or need personalized advice, consider seeking guidance from a qualified financial advisor. An advisor can help you develop an investment plan tailored to your goals, risk tolerance, and financial situation.

Beginners may start investing with confidence and position themselves for long-term financial success by adhering to these straightforward investing techniques. Recall that investing is a marathon, not a sprint, and that long-term financial success requires patience and discipline.

CHAPTER 7: RETIREMENT PLANNING

Retirement planning is a critical aspect of financial management that involves setting goals, making strategic decisions, and taking actions to ensure a secure and comfortable retirement. Whether you're just starting your career or nearing retirement age, proactive retirement planning is essential for achieving financial independence and enjoying your golden years.

Importance Of Retirement Planning

While retirement may seem distant for some, proactive planning early on is essential for achicving financial independence and peace of mind in retirement. Here's why retirement planning is of paramount importance:

1. Financial Security in Retirement:
Retirement planning provides the financial security needed to sustain your lifestyle and cover expenses during retirement. By saving and investing strategically, you can build a nest egg that generates a steady stream of income to support your needs and aspirations in retirement.

2. Mitigating the Risk of Outliving Savings:
With increasing life expectancy, the risk of outliving your savings in retirement is a significant concern. Retirement planning helps you estimate your future expenses, determine your retirement savings target, and ensure you have adequate resources to maintain your standard of living throughout your retirement years.

3. Maintaining Independence and Autonomy:
Effective retirement planning empowers you to maintain your independence and autonomy in retirement. By taking control of financial futures, retirees can make informed decisions

about how they want to live, where they want to reside, and what activities they want to pursue during retirement.

4. Addressing Healthcare Costs:
Healthcare expenses tend to increase with age, making it essential to plan for medical costs in retirement. Retirement planning allows you to budget for healthcare expenses, explore insurance options, and allocate resources to cover potential medical needs, thereby minimizing the financial burden of healthcare in retirement.

5. Achieving Retirement Goals and Aspirations:
Retirement planning enables you to identify your retirement goals and aspirations and take the necessary steps to achieve them. Whether it's traveling the world, pursuing hobbies, volunteering, or spending time with family, retirement planning ensures that you can fulfill your dreams and aspirations in retirement.

6. Minimizing Financial Stress:
Effective retirement planning reduces financial stress and anxiety by providing a roadmap for achieving financial security in retirement. Knowing that you have a well-thought-out plan in place can alleviate concerns about running out of money or being unprepared for unexpected expenses during retirement.

7. Maximizing Retirement Benefits and Resources:
Retirement planning allows you to maximize your retirement benefits and resources, such as employer-sponsored retirement plans, Social Security benefits, pension income, and personal savings. By optimizing these resources, you can enhance your financial well-being and make the most of your retirement years.

8. Leaving a Legacy for Future Generations:
Retirement planning enables you to leave a legacy for your loved ones and future

generations. By managing finances prudently and preserving wealth, retirees can pass on assets, financial wisdom, and a legacy of financial responsibility to their heirs.

To achieve financial stability, freedom, and peace of mind in retirement, retirement planning is crucial. You can make sure you have the means and freedom to live a happy and comfortable retirement by intentionally saving for it and being ready for it. It's never too early or late to start retirement planning and take charge of your financial destiny, regardless of when you're starting your work or approaching retirement age.

Types Of Retirement Accounts

Retirement accounts are specialized investment vehicles designed to help you save and invest for retirement while enjoying various tax benefits. Understanding the different types of retirement accounts available can help you choose the best option based on your financial goals, employment status, and tax situation. Here are some common types of retirement accounts:

1. 401(k) Plans:
401(k) plans are employer-sponsored retirement accounts offered by many private sector employers. Employees can contribute a portion of their pre-tax income to their 401(k) accounts, which are then invested in a selection of investment options chosen by the employer. Contributions to a traditional 401(k) are tax-deferred, meaning they are not subject to income tax until withdrawn in retirement.

2. Individual Retirement Accounts (IRAs):
IRAs are retirement accounts that individuals can open and contribute to independently of their employer. There are two main types of IRAs:
- Traditional IRA: Contributions to a traditional IRA may be tax-deductible, and earnings grow tax-deferred until withdrawal in retirement. Withdrawals are taxed as ordinary income in retirement.

- Roth IRA: Contributions to a Roth IRA are made with after-tax dollars, meaning contributions are not tax-deductible. However, qualified withdrawals, including earnings, are tax-free in retirement, provided certain conditions are met.

3. Roth 401(k) Plans:
Roth 401(k) plans combine features of traditional 401(k) plans and Roth IRAs. Employees contribute after-tax dollars to their Roth 401(k) accounts, and withdrawals in retirement are tax-free, including earnings, if certain conditions are met. Not all employers offer Roth 401(k) plans, but they are becoming increasingly popular.

4. SEP IRAs (Simplified Employee Pension IRAs):
SEP IRAs are retirement accounts available to self-employed individuals and small business owners. Employers can contribute to SEP IRAs on behalf of eligible employees, including themselves, up to certain limits. Contributions

are tax-deductible, and earnings grow tax-deferred until withdrawal in retirement.

5. SIMPLE IRAs (Savings Incentive Match Plan for Employees IRAs):

SIMPLE IRAs are retirement plans designed for small businesses with fewer than 100 employees. Both employers and employees can contribute to SIMPLE IRAs. Employer contributions are tax-deductible, and employee contributions are made on a pre-tax basis. Withdrawals in retirement are taxed as ordinary income.

6. Thrift Savings Plan (TSP):

The Thrift Savings Plan is a retirement savings plan available to federal employees and members of the uniformed services. Contributions to TSP accounts are made on a pre-tax or after-tax basis, depending on the type of TSP account (traditional or Roth). TSP offers a variety of investment options and tax benefits similar to 401(k) plans.

7. Pension Plans:

Pension plans, also known as defined benefit plans, are retirement plans sponsored by employers that provide guaranteed income to employees in retirement. Pension benefits are based on factors such as years of service and salary history. While less common today, some employers still offer pension plans to their employees.

8. Deferred Compensation Plans:

Deferred compensation plans, such as 457(b) plans for governmental employers and 403(b) plans for certain non-profit organizations and educational institutions, allow employees to defer a portion of their compensation to retirement accounts. Contributions are tax-deferred, and withdrawals in retirement are taxed as ordinary income.

You may save and invest for retirement more wisely if you are aware of the features, eligibility requirements, and tax ramifications of the many types of retirement accounts. When choosing the best retirement plan for your financial requirements and objectives, it's critical to take into account elements including job benefits, contribution caps, investment possibilities, and tax advantages.

Strategies For Maximizing Retirement Savings And Achieving Financial Independence

Achieving financial independence and building a sufficient retirement nest egg requires careful planning, disciplined saving, and strategic investment. By implementing effective strategies, you can maximize your retirement savings and work towards achieving financial independence. Here are some key strategies to consider:

1. Start Saving Early:
Time is a crucial factor in retirement savings due to the power of compounding. Start saving for retirement as early as possible to take advantage

of compounding returns and allow your investments to grow over time.

2. Take Advantage of Employer-Sponsored Plans:

Participate in employer-sponsored retirement plans such as 401(k), 403(b), or Thrift Savings Plan (TSP), if available. Contribute enough to take full advantage of any employer matching contributions, as this is essentially free money that boosts your retirement savings.

3. Maximize Contributions to Tax-Advantaged Accounts:

Contribute the maximum allowable amount to tax-advantaged retirement accounts such as IRAs, Roth IRAs, and employer-sponsored plans. Maxing out your contributions allows you to take full advantage of tax benefits and accelerate your retirement savings growth.

4. Automate Savings and Investments:

Set up automatic contributions to your retirement accounts directly from your paycheck or bank account. Automating your savings ensures consistency and eliminates the temptation to spend money that could otherwise be saved for retirement.

5. Reduce Expenses and Increase Savings Rate:
Evaluate your expenses and identify areas where you can cut back to increase your savings rate. Redirect any surplus funds towards retirement savings to accelerate your progress towards financial independence.

6. Diversify Your Investments:
Diversify your retirement portfolio across different asset classes, such as stocks, bonds, and real estate, to spread risk and optimize returns. Avoid putting all your eggs in one basket and regularly rebalance your portfolio to maintain your desired asset allocation.

7. Invest Wisely and Minimize Fees:
Invest in low-cost, diversified investment options such as index funds and exchange-traded

funds (ETFs) to minimize fees and expenses. High fees can eat into your investment returns over time, so choose investment vehicles with competitive fees and expenses.

8. Take Advantage of Catch-Up Contributions:
Individuals age 50 and older can make additional catch-up contributions to retirement accounts above the standard contribution limits. Take advantage of catch-up contributions to accelerate your retirement savings in the years leading up to retirement.

9. Continuously Educate Yourself:
Stay informed about retirement planning, investment strategies, and personal finance topics. Continuously educate yourself through books, online resources, seminars, and workshops to make informed decisions and optimize your retirement savings strategy.

10. Develop Multiple Streams of Income:

Explore opportunities to generate additional income streams outside of traditional employment, such as rental income, freelance work, passive investments, or entrepreneurship. Developing multiple income streams can supplement your retirement savings and provide financial flexibility in retirement.

11. Create a Comprehensive Financial Plan:
Develop a comprehensive financial plan that encompasses retirement goals, budgeting, debt management, investment strategy, risk management, and estate planning. A well-rounded financial plan provides a roadmap for achieving financial independence and retiring comfortably.

12. Seek Professional Guidance if Needed:
Consider working with a qualified financial advisor or retirement planning specialist to develop a personalized retirement savings strategy tailored to your unique circumstances, goals, and risk tolerance. An advisor can provide expert guidance, help you navigate complex

financial decisions, and optimize your path towards financial independence.

You may optimize your savings potential, attain financial independence, and have a pleasant retirement lifestyle by putting these techniques into practice and maintaining a disciplined attitude to retirement savings. Recall that obtaining financial independence is a path that calls for perseverance, forethought, and proactive preparation, but the benefits of stability and financial freedom in retirement are priceless.

CHAPTER 8: REAL ESTATE AND PASSIVE INCOME

Real estate investment is a powerful wealth-building strategy that offers the potential for generating passive income and long-term capital appreciation. By investing in rental properties, you can create a steady stream of passive income while building equity and wealth over time.

Exploring Real Estate Investment Opportunities

Real estate investment offers you a variety of opportunities to build wealth, generate passive income, and diversify your investment portfolios. Whether you're a novice investor or a seasoned entrepreneur, exploring real estate investment opportunities can provide numerous benefits and avenues for financial growth. Here's how to get started:

1. Define Your Investment Goals:
Before diving into real estate investment, clarify your investment goals and objectives. Determine whether you're looking to generate passive income, build equity through property appreciation, diversify your investment portfolio, or achieve long-term financial independence. Your goals will help guide your investment strategy and decision-making process.

2. Assess Your Risk Tolerance:
Evaluate your risk tolerance and comfort level with real estate investment. Consider factors such as your financial situation, investment experience, time horizon, and willingness to take on risks. Real estate investment involves various risks, including market fluctuations, property vacancies, tenant issues, and unexpected expenses, so it's essential to assess your risk tolerance before proceeding.

3. Educate Yourself:

Take the time to educate yourself about the fundamentals of real estate investment, including property types, financing options, market analysis, property management, and legal considerations. There are plenty of resources available, including books, online courses, seminars, and networking events, that can help you develop a solid understanding of real estate investment principles.

4. Identify Investment Strategies:

Explore different real estate investment strategies and determine which approach aligns best with your goals and preferences. Common investment strategies include:

- Rental Properties: Purchase residential or commercial properties and rent them out to tenants to generate rental income.
- Fix and Flip: Purchase distressed properties, renovate them, and sell them for a profit.
- Real Estate Investment Trusts (REITs): Invest in publicly traded REITs, which

own and manage income-generating properties such as office buildings, shopping centers, and apartment complexes.
- Real Estate Crowdfunding: Participate in real estate crowdfunding platforms that allow investors to pool their funds to invest in properties or real estate projects.

5. Conduct Market Research:

Research local real estate markets to identify investment opportunities and trends. Analyze factors such as supply and demand dynamics, property prices, rental yields, economic indicators, job growth, population trends, and infrastructure development. Understanding market conditions will help you make informed decisions about where to invest and when to enter or exit the market.

6. Perform Due Diligence:

Thoroughly evaluate potential investment properties before making a purchase decision. Conduct due diligence on property condition, location, rental potential, cash flow projections, financing options, zoning regulations, property taxes, and potential risks. Engage with real estate professionals, such as real estate agents, appraisers, inspectors, and attorneys, to assist you in the due diligence process.

7. Secure Financing:
Determine your financing options and secure funding for your real estate investments. Explore mortgage options, private lenders, hard money lenders, seller financing, and other sources of financing to finance property acquisitions. Consider factors such as interest rates, loan terms, down payment requirements, and closing costs when evaluating financing options.

8. Network and Build Relationships:
Network with other real estate investors, industry professionals, and local community members to expand your knowledge, exchange ideas, and identify potential investment opportunities. Building relationships with real estate agents, property managers, contractors,

lenders, and other professionals can provide valuable insights and resources to support your real estate investment endeavors.

9. Develop an Investment Plan:
Create a comprehensive investment plan that outlines your investment goals, target markets, investment criteria, acquisition criteria, financing strategies, risk management strategies, and exit strategies. Having a clear investment plan will help you stay focused, disciplined, and organized as you pursue real estate investment opportunities.

10. Take Action and Monitor Progress:
Once you've identified suitable investment opportunities, take action and execute your investment plan. Monitor the performance of your investments regularly, track key metrics such as rental income, expenses, occupancy rates, and property appreciation, and make adjustments to your investment strategy as needed to optimize returns and mitigate risks.

Investigating real estate investing prospects may be a thrilling and fulfilling undertaking that offers you the chance to accumulate wealth, produce passive income, and eventually become financially independent. Investors may find profitable real estate investment options that fit with their financial objectives and desires by following these procedures and doing extensive research and due diligence.

Generating Passive Income Streams

Passive income streams are an essential component of financial independence, providing you with the ability to generate income without actively trading your time for money. By establishing passive income streams, you can create a steady source of income that requires minimal ongoing effort, allowing them to enjoy greater flexibility, security, and freedom in your life. Here are several strategies for generating passive income streams:

1. Rental Income from Real Estate:
Real estate investment offers the opportunity to earn passive income through rental properties. By purchasing residential or commercial properties and renting them out to tenants, investors can generate a consistent stream of rental income. Hiring a property management company can further reduce the active involvement required, making real estate a truly passive income stream.

2. Dividend Stocks and Bonds:
Investing in dividend-paying stocks and bonds can provide a reliable source of passive income. Dividend stocks pay out regular dividends to shareholders, while bonds pay interest income to bondholders. By building a diversified portfolio of dividend stocks and bonds, investors can create a stream of passive income that grows over time.

3. Royalties from Intellectual Property:

Creating and licensing intellectual property such as books, music, patents, or software can generate passive income through royalties. Once the intellectual property is created, the creator can earn royalties from sales or licensing agreements without requiring ongoing effort or time investment.

4. Peer-to-Peer Lending:
Peer-to-peer lending platforms allow you to lend money to borrowers in exchange for interest payments. By investing in peer-to-peer lending, investors can earn passive income from interest payments without the need for active management or oversight.

5. Affiliate Marketing:
Affiliate marketing involves promoting products or services through affiliate links and earning a commission on sales generated through those links. By building a website, blog, or social media presence and partnering with affiliate programs, you can earn passive income from affiliate commissions.

6. Rental Income from Equipment or Vehicles:

Renting out equipment, such as tools, machinery, or vehicles, can generate passive income for owners. Businesses or individuals in need of temporary access to equipment may be willing to pay rental fees, providing a passive income stream for equipment owners.

7. Real Estate Investment Trusts (REITs):

Real estate investment trusts (REITs) allow investors to invest in income-generating real estate properties without directly owning or managing them. REITs typically distribute a significant portion of their rental income to shareholders in the form of dividends, providing investors with a passive income stream from real estate investments.

8. Online Courses or Membership Sites:

Creating and selling online courses or membership sites can generate passive income for instructors or content creators. Once the course or membership site is created, it can be marketed and sold to customers, generating ongoing revenue without requiring active involvement.

9. High-Yield Savings Accounts or Certificates of Deposit (CDs):
While not as high as other passive income streams, interest earned from high-yield savings accounts or CDs can provide a low-risk source of passive income. By depositing funds into a high-yield savings account or CD, you can earn interest on your savings without the need for active management.

10. Automated Business Systems:
Building automated business systems or online businesses that generate revenue through e-commerce, advertising, subscriptions, or digital products can create passive income streams. By leveraging automation, outsourcing, and technology, you can generate income with minimal ongoing effort.

Although creating passive income streams takes time, patience, and work up front, the long-term advantages of financial freedom and independence make the initial outlay worthwhile. You may establish a route to financial independence and accomplish your objectives of passive income and wealth accumulation by diversifying your sources of income, utilizing technology and automation, and concentrating on developing scalable and sustainable passive income streams.

Tips For Successful Real Estate Investing

Real estate investing offers you the opportunity to build wealth, generate passive income, and achieve financial independence. However, successful real estate investing requires careful planning, diligent research, and strategic decision-making. Whether you're a novice investor or a seasoned pro, here are some tips to help you succeed in real estate investing:

1. Set Clear Investment Goals:
Define your investment goals and objectives before diving into real estate investing. Determine whether you're looking to generate passive income, build equity through property appreciation, diversify your investment portfolio, or achieve long-term financial independence. Having clear goals will guide your investment strategy and help you stay focused on your objectives.

2. Conduct Thorough Market Research:
Research local real estate markets to identify investment opportunities and trends. Analyze factors such as supply and demand dynamics, property prices, rental yields, economic indicators, job growth, population trends, and infrastructure development. Understanding market conditions will help you make informed

decisions about where to invest and when to enter or exit the market.

3. Know Your Budget and Financing Options: Determine your budget and financing options before starting your property search. Calculate how much you can afford to invest, including down payment, closing costs, and ongoing expenses such as mortgage payments, property taxes, insurance, and maintenance. Explore financing options such as traditional mortgages, private lenders, hard money loans, seller financing, or partnerships.

4. Perform Due Diligence on Properties: Thoroughly evaluate potential investment properties before making a purchase decision. Conduct due diligence on property condition, location, rental potential, cash flow projections, financing options, zoning regulations, property taxes, and potential risks. Engage with real estate professionals, such as real estate agents, appraisers, inspectors, and attorneys, to assist you in the due diligence process.

5. Invest for Cash Flow and Long-Term Appreciation:

Focus on investing in properties that generate positive cash flow and have the potential for long-term appreciation. Look for properties with strong rental demand, stable occupancy rates, and potential for value appreciation over time. Avoid speculative investments or properties with negative cash flow unless you have a clear strategy for turning them around.

6. Diversify Your Real Estate Portfolio:

Diversification is key to reducing risk and maximizing returns in real estate investing. Consider diversifying your portfolio across different property types, locations, and investment strategies. By spreading your investments across a variety of assets, you can mitigate the impact of market fluctuations and minimize exposure to specific risks.

7. Build a Reliable Network of Professionals:
Surround yourself with a team of experienced real estate professionals, including real estate agents, property managers, contractors, lenders, attorneys, and accountants. Building a reliable network of professionals will provide you with access to expertise, resources, and support throughout the investment process, from acquisition to management and beyond.

8. Stay Informed and Continuously Educate Yourself:
Real estate markets are constantly evolving, so it's essential to stay informed and continuously educate yourself about industry trends, regulations, and best practices. Attend real estate seminars, workshops, networking events, and conferences to expand your knowledge, learn from experts, and stay ahead of the curve.

9. Practice Patience and Discipline:
Real estate investing is a long-term endeavor that requires patience, discipline, and resilience.

Avoid making impulsive decisions or chasing quick profits. Stick to your investment plan, conduct thorough research, and be prepared to weather market fluctuations and challenges along the way.

10. Monitor and Evaluate Your Investments Regularly:
Monitor the performance of your real estate investments regularly and evaluate your financial metrics, such as rental income, expenses, occupancy rates, cash flow, and property appreciation. Assess the effectiveness of your investment strategy, make adjustments as needed, and be prepared to exit underperforming investments if necessary.

In the exciting and lucrative world of real estate investing, you may increase your chances of success and reach your financial objectives by heeding their advice and taking a methodical, educated approach to the process.

CHAPTER 9: PROTECTING YOUR WEALTH

Building wealth requires diligent effort, but protecting it is equally important to ensure long-term financial security and stability. Whether you've accumulated wealth through investments, business ventures, inheritance, or other means, safeguarding your assets from risks and threats is essential.

Understanding Insurance Coverage

Insurance coverage plays a crucial role in safeguarding individuals and families against unforeseen risks and financial hardships. Whether it's protecting your health, life, property, or income, insurance provides financial security and peace of mind in the face of adversity. Here's a comprehensive overview of various types of insurance coverage:

1. Health Insurance:

Health insurance covers medical expenses and provides financial protection against the high costs of healthcare services, including hospitalization, surgeries, doctor visits, prescription drugs, and preventive care. Health insurance plans vary in coverage levels, cost-sharing arrangements, and provider networks, with options such as employer-sponsored health plans, individual health plans, government-sponsored plans like Medicare and Medicaid, and marketplace exchange plans under the Affordable Care Act (ACA).

2. Life Insurance:

Life insurance provides financial protection to beneficiaries in the event of the insured's death. It pays out a lump sum death benefit to designated beneficiaries, typically family members or dependents, to help cover expenses such as funeral costs, outstanding debts, mortgage payments, and living expenses. There are various types of life insurance, including term life insurance, whole life insurance, universal life insurance, and variable life insurance, each with different features, benefits, and premium structures.

3. Property Insurance:

Property insurance protects against damage or loss to physical property, including homes, rental properties, commercial buildings, and personal belongings. Property insurance policies typically cover perils such as fire, theft, vandalism, natural disasters (e.g., hurricanes, earthquakes), and liability claims. Common types of property insurance include homeowners insurance, renters insurance, landlord insurance, condominium insurance, and commercial property insurance.

4. Auto Insurance:

Auto insurance provides financial protection against damage or loss to vehicles and liability for bodily injury or property damage resulting from automobile accidents. Auto insurance policies typically include coverage for property damage liability, bodily injury liability, collision coverage, comprehensive coverage, uninsured/underinsured motorist coverage, and personal injury protection (PIP) or medical payments coverage.

5. Disability Insurance:
Disability insurance replaces a portion of your income if you become unable to work due to a disabling illness or injury. It provides financial protection against the loss of income and helps cover ongoing living expenses, including mortgage or rent payments, utilities, groceries, and medical bills. Disability insurance can be obtained through employer-sponsored disability plans, private disability insurance policies, or government disability programs such as Social Security Disability Insurance (SSDI).

6. Liability Insurance:
Liability insurance protects individuals and businesses from financial losses arising from legal claims and lawsuits for bodily injury or property damage caused to others. It provides coverage for legal defense costs, settlements,

and judgments resulting from covered claims. Common types of liability insurance include general liability insurance, professional liability insurance (errors and omissions insurance), product liability insurance, and umbrella liability insurance.

7. Long-Term Care Insurance:
Long-term care insurance covers the costs of long-term care services, including nursing home care, assisted living facilities, and in-home care, for individuals who require assistance with activities of daily living (ADLs) due to chronic illness, disability, or cognitive impairment. Long-term care insurance helps protect assets and preserve financial independence by covering the high costs of long-term care services that may not be covered by health insurance or government programs like Medicare.

8. Business Insurance:
Business insurance provides financial protection to businesses against various risks and liabilities associated with operating a business. It includes

coverage for property damage, liability claims, business interruption, worker's compensation, professional liability, cyber liability, and other specific risks faced by businesses in different industries. Business insurance helps businesses mitigate financial losses and maintain continuity in the face of unexpected events.

It's critical to comprehend insurance coverage in order to safeguard your financial stability and reduce hazards in a variety of spheres of your existence. You may guarantee complete financial security and peace of mind for yourself and your loved ones by assessing your insurance needs, weighing your coverage alternatives, and choosing suitable insurance products catered to your unique situation. It's important to keep in mind to examine your insurance coverage on a regular basis, update your policies when necessary, and speak with insurance specialists about any queries or worries you may have regarding your needs and available coverage alternatives.

Estate Planning And Asset Protection Strategies

Estate planning and asset protection are essential components of financial planning that help individuals and families protect their assets, minimize taxes, and ensure the orderly transfer of wealth to future generations. By implementing effective estate planning and asset protection strategies, you can safeguard your assets from creditors, lawsuits, probate, and other potential risks while preserving your wealth and legacy. Here are some key strategies for estate planning and asset protection:

1. Create a Comprehensive Estate Plan:
Develop a comprehensive estate plan that outlines your wishes for the distribution of your assets and the management of your affairs in the event of incapacity or death. Work with an experienced estate planning attorney to draft essential documents such as wills, trusts, powers of attorney, healthcare directives, and beneficiary designations to ensure your estate is

managed according to your wishes and to minimize taxes and probate costs.

2. Establish Trusts:
Trusts are powerful estate planning tools that allow you to protect assets, minimize taxes, and control the distribution of wealth to beneficiaries. Establishing trusts such as revocable living trusts, irrevocable trusts, charitable trusts, and asset protection trusts can provide flexibility, privacy, and asset protection benefits. Trusts can help shield assets from creditors, avoid probate, and ensure the efficient transfer of wealth to future generations.

3. Utilize Asset Protection Entities:
Consider utilizing legal entities such as limited liability companies (LLCs), limited partnerships (LPs), and corporations to hold and protect assets from potential liabilities and lawsuits. These entities offer liability protection by separating personal assets from business or investment assets, shielding them from creditors and legal claims. Properly structuring and

maintaining these entities can enhance asset protection and minimize risks.

4. Maximize Retirement Accounts and Benefits:
Take advantage of tax-advantaged retirement accounts such as 401(k) plans, individual retirement accounts (IRAs), and pension plans to maximize retirement savings and minimize taxes. Retirement accounts offer creditor protection benefits under federal law, shielding assets from creditors and lawsuits in certain circumstances. Consider contributing to retirement accounts regularly and optimizing investment strategies to build wealth and protect assets for retirement.

5. Review and Update Beneficiary Designations:
Regularly review and update beneficiary designations on financial accounts, retirement accounts, life insurance policies, and other assets to ensure they align with your estate planning goals and intentions. Designating beneficiaries

properly can help avoid probate, streamline asset transfer, and provide asset protection benefits for heirs and beneficiaries.

6. Purchase Adequate Insurance Coverage:
Maintain adequate insurance coverage to protect against potential risks and liabilities, including homeowners insurance, renters insurance, automobile insurance, umbrella insurance, professional liability insurance, and long-term care insurance. Insurance policies provide financial protection against property damage, liability claims, personal injury, disability, and other unforeseen events, helping to safeguard assets and mitigate risks.

7. Implement Gifting and Wealth Transfer Strategies:
Implement gifting strategies such as annual gift tax exclusions, lifetime gift tax exemptions, and charitable giving to transfer wealth to heirs and beneficiaries tax-efficiently and reduce the size of the taxable estate. Gifting assets during your lifetime can help minimize estate taxes, provide

financial assistance to loved ones, and support charitable causes while preserving assets for future generations.

8. Consider Asset Protection Trusts:
Asset protection trusts are specialized trusts designed to shield assets from creditors and legal claims while allowing you to retain some degree of control and access to trust assets. Domestic asset protection trusts (DAPTs) and offshore asset protection trusts (OAPTs) offer varying levels of asset protection benefits and legal protections, depending on jurisdictional laws and regulations.

9. Plan for Incapacity:
Plan for incapacity by establishing advance directives such as durable powers of attorney, healthcare proxies, and living wills to appoint trusted persons to make financial and healthcare decisions on your behalf in the event of incapacity. Having comprehensive incapacity planning documents in place ensures that your affairs are managed according to your wishes

and best interests if you become unable to make decisions for yourself.

10. Seek Professional Guidance and Review Regularly:
Work with experienced professionals, including estate planning attorneys, financial advisors, tax advisors, and insurance specialists, to develop and implement a comprehensive estate plan and asset protection strategy tailored to your specific needs and circumstances. Regularly review and update your estate plan and asset protection strategies as your financial situation, family dynamics, and laws change over time to ensure they remain effective and aligned with your goals and objectives.

Importance Of Having A Will And Healthcare Directive

Having a will and healthcare directive is essential for everyone, regardless of age, wealth, or health status. These legal documents provide instructions for how you want your assets to be distributed and your medical care to be managed in the event of incapacity or death. Here's why having a will and healthcare directive is crucial:

1. Ensures Your Wishes are Followed:
A will allows you to specify how you want your assets to be distributed after your death. Without a will, state laws dictate how your assets will be distributed, which may not align with your wishes. Similarly, a healthcare directive (also known as a living will or advance directive) outlines your preferences for medical treatment and end-of-life care if you become incapacitated and unable to communicate your wishes.

2. Protects Your Loved Ones:
A will enables you to designate guardians for minor children, ensuring they are cared for by trusted persons if you pass away prematurely. It also minimizes family disputes and legal battles over inheritance by clearly outlining your wishes for asset distribution. A healthcare directive relieves your loved ones of the burden of making

difficult medical decisions on your behalf by providing guidance on your healthcare preferences.

3. Avoids Intestacy Laws:
Intestacy laws govern how assets are distributed when someone dies without a will. These laws vary by state and may result in assets being distributed in a way that does not reflect your wishes or preferences. By having a will, you retain control over how your assets are distributed and avoid intestacy laws dictating the outcome.

4. Facilitates Estate Administration:
A will simplifies the probate process by appointing an executor to oversee the administration of your estate. The executor is responsible for gathering assets, paying debts and taxes, and distributing assets to beneficiaries according to the terms of the will. Without a will, the probate process can be more complex and time-consuming, leading to delays and additional expenses.

5. Provides Clarity and Certainty:

Having a will and healthcare directive provides clarity and certainty for you and your loved ones during challenging times. It ensures that your wishes are known and respected, reducing confusion, stress, and disagreements among family members. It also gives you peace of mind knowing that your affairs are in order and your loved ones will be taken care of according to your wishes.

6. Allows for Customization:

A will and healthcare directive allow for customization based on your unique circumstances and preferences. You can specify how you want your assets to be distributed, appoint specific persons to handle your affairs, and provide detailed instructions for medical care and end-of-life decisions. This customization ensures that your wishes are accurately reflected and carried out.

7. Addresses Complex Family Situations:

For people in blended families, people with children from previous marriages, or those with complex family dynamics, a will is especially important. It enables you to address unique family situations, provide for all family members, and prevent conflicts or disputes among heirs. A healthcare directive also allows you to appoint a healthcare proxy to make medical decisions on your behalf, ensuring your preferences are respected, even in complex family situations.

8. Offers Peace of Mind:

Ultimately, having a will and healthcare directive offers peace of mind knowing that your affairs are in order and your wishes will be honored. It provides reassurance that your loved ones will be taken care of according to your wishes, both financially and medically, and reduces the burden on family members during difficult times. By proactively planning for the future, you can alleviate stress and uncertainty for yourself and your loved ones.

You need a will and healthcare directive to ensure that your wishes are carried out, your loved ones are protected, and your affairs are handled in line with your decisions. These contracts provide clarity, certainty, and peace of mind, which are crucial for careful estate planning and healthcare decision-making. To protect yourself and your loved ones, you should be proactive and draft a will and healthcare directive. Consult an estate planning lawyer and begin drafting these crucial documents as soon as possible.

CHAPTER 10: FINANCIAL LITERACY FOR LONG-TERM SUCCESS

Financial literacy is the foundation of long-term financial success and stability. It encompasses the knowledge, skills, and attitudes needed to make informed financial decisions, manage money effectively, and achieve financial goals. By becoming financially literate, you can take control of your finances, build wealth, and secure your financial future.

Continuous Learning And Staying Informed About Personal Finance

In today's rapidly changing financial landscape, continuous learning and staying informed about personal finance are essential for you to navigate complex financial decisions, manage money effectively, and achieve your financial goals. By prioritizing financial education and remaining proactive in staying informed, you can empower yourself to make informed decisions, adapt to changing circumstances, and secure your financial well-being. Here's why continuous learning and staying informed about personal finance are crucial:

1. Keeping Up With Evolving Financial Trends:
Financial markets, products, and regulations are constantly evolving, making it essential for you to stay informed about the latest trends and developments in personal finance. By staying abreast of changes in interest rates, investment opportunities, tax laws, and economic indicators, you can make informed decisions and adapt your financial strategies accordingly.

2. Adapting to Changing Life Circumstances:
Life is full of changes, from starting a new job and buying a home to getting married, having children, and planning for retirement. Staying informed about personal finance allows you to adapt to changing life circumstances and make adjustments to your financial plans as needed.

Whether it's updating insurance coverage, revising investment allocations, or revisiting estate planning documents, continuous learning enables you to stay proactive and responsive to life events.

3. Maximizing Financial Opportunities:
Staying informed about personal finance opens doors to new opportunities for wealth accumulation, asset growth, and financial optimization. By learning about different investment vehicles, tax-saving strategies, and financial products, you can identify opportunities to maximize returns, minimize taxes, and optimize your financial situation. Continuous learning enables you to make strategic decisions that align with your goals and aspirations.

4. Avoiding Financial Pitfalls and Scams:
Financial literacy empowers you to recognize and avoid common financial pitfalls, scams, and fraudulent schemes that can jeopardize your financial well-being. By staying informed about

red flags, warning signs, and common tactics used by scammers, you can protect yourself and your assets from financial harm. Continuous learning enables you to make informed decisions and avoid falling victim to financial fraud or exploitation.

5. Empowering Financial Independence and Freedom:
Continuous learning about personal finance is a key enabler of financial independence and freedom. By acquiring knowledge about budgeting, saving, investing, and wealth-building strategies, you can take control of your finances, reduce dependence on others, and create opportunities for financial autonomy. Staying informed empowers you to pursue your goals, live life on your own terms, and achieve greater financial security and freedom.

6. Fostering a Growth Mindset and Personal Development:
Continuous learning fosters a growth mindset and personal development, encouraging you to

seek out new knowledge, skills, and experiences. By expanding your financial literacy and capabilities, you can enhance your confidence, competence, and resilience in managing money and navigating financial challenges. Staying informed about personal finance fuels personal growth and empowers you to reach your full potential.

7. Building Resilience and Preparedness:
Staying informed about personal finance helps you build resilience and preparedness to withstand financial shocks, emergencies, and unexpected events. By learning about emergency savings, insurance coverage, and risk management strategies, you can mitigate financial risks and prepare for unforeseen circumstances. Continuous learning instills a sense of preparedness and confidence in facing financial challenges head-on.

8. Setting a Positive Example for Future Generations:

By prioritizing continuous learning and staying informed about personal finance, you set a positive example for future generations and inspire others to take charge of your financial futures. Whether it's teaching children about money management, mentoring younger colleagues in the workplace, or sharing financial knowledge with friends and family, continuous learning fosters a culture of financial empowerment and responsibility.

For you to successfully navigate the complicated financial environment of today, make wise decisions, and reach your financial objectives, you must never stop studying and remain up to date on personal finance. Through investing in lifelong learning, financial education, and proactive information gathering, you may empower yourself to accumulate wealth, safeguard your financial future, and prosper in a constantly evolving global environment.

Resources For Improving Financial Literacy

Improving financial literacy is a journey that requires access to reliable information, educational resources, and practical tools to enhance your understanding of personal finance concepts and principles. Fortunately, there are numerous resources available to help you improve your financial literacy and make informed decisions about money management, investing, budgeting, and more. Here are some valuable resources for improving financial literacy:

1. Personal Finance Websites and Blogs:
Explore reputable personal finance websites and blogs that offer a wealth of articles, guides, and resources on various financial topics. Websites like Investopedia, NerdWallet, The Balance, and Kiplinger provide comprehensive information on budgeting, saving, investing, retirement planning, debt management, and more.

Subscribe to newsletters or RSS feeds to stay updated on the latest articles and insights.

2. Financial Literacy Courses and Workshops:
Enroll in financial literacy courses, workshops, and seminars offered by reputable institutions, universities, community colleges, and nonprofit organizations. Many organizations offer online courses and workshops on topics such as basic money management, investing fundamentals, retirement planning, and debt reduction. Look for courses that are taught by certified financial planners or accredited financial educators for high-quality instruction.

3. Online Financial Tools and Calculators:
Take advantage of online financial tools and calculators to assess your financial situation, set financial goals, and make informed decisions. Websites like Mint, Personal Capital, and YNAB (You Need a Budget) offer free budgeting tools, expense trackers, retirement calculators, investment calculators, debt payoff calculators,

and other valuable resources to help you manage your finances effectively.

4. Financial Podcasts and Webinars:
Listen to financial podcasts and webinars hosted by industry experts, financial advisors, and thought leaders to gain insights and practical tips on personal finance topics. Podcasts such as "The Dave Ramsey Show," "The Clark Howard Podcast," "The Suze Orman Show," and "The Mad Fientist Podcast" cover a wide range of financial topics, including budgeting, investing, debt management, and retirement planning.

5. Books on Personal Finance:
Read books on personal finance written by renowned authors and experts in the field. Books such as "The Total Money Makeover" by Dave Ramsey, "Rich Dad Poor Dad" by Robert Kiyosaki, "The Millionaire Next Door" by Thomas J. Stanley and William D. Danko, and "The Bogleheads' Guide to Investing" by Taylor Larimore, Mel Lindauer, and Michael LeBoeuf

offer valuable insights and strategies for improving financial literacy and building wealth.

6. Government and Nonprofit Resources:
Explore government and nonprofit resources dedicated to financial education and literacy. Websites like MyMoney.gov (U.S. government's financial literacy website), Consumer Financial Protection Bureau (CFPB), Federal Trade Commission (FTC), and National Endowment for Financial Education (NEFE) offer educational materials, tools, and resources to help consumers make informed financial decisions and avoid scams and fraud.

7. Online Forums and Communities:
Join online forums and communities focused on personal finance, where you can ask questions, share experiences, and learn from others' insights and perspectives. Platforms like Reddit's personal finance subreddit (r/personalfinance), Bogleheads forum, and The White Coat Investor forum provide valuable advice, support, and guidance on a wide range of financial topics,

from investing strategies to debt repayment techniques.

8. Financial Apps and Mobile Tools:
Download financial apps and mobile tools that offer convenient ways to manage your money, track expenses, and monitor your financial progress. Apps like Acorns, Robinhood, Stash, and Betterment provide user-friendly interfaces, automated savings features, investment options, and educational resources to help you achieve your financial goals on the go.

9. Financial Planning Professionals:
Consider seeking guidance from certified financial planners (CFPs), financial advisors, or fee-only planners who can provide personalized advice and guidance tailored to your specific financial situation and goals. Working with a financial professional can help you develop a comprehensive financial plan, optimize your investment portfolio, and make informed decisions about your finances.

10. Continuing Education and Lifelong Learning:

Finally, commit to ongoing education and lifelong learning to continually improve your financial literacy and stay informed about changes in the financial landscape. Attend conferences, webinars, and seminars, participate in online courses and workshops, read books and articles regularly, and seek out new opportunities to expand your knowledge and skills in personal finance.

You can improve your financial literacy, make wise decisions, and take charge of your financial destiny by utilizing these tools and making a commitment to lifelong learning. It's important to keep in mind that increasing financial literacy is a journey, so exercise patience, maintain your curiosity, and seize each chance you get to learn and advance.

Building A Mindset For Long-term Financial Success

Achieving long-term financial success requires more than just practical knowledge of money management techniques and investment strategies. It also demands a mindset characterized by discipline, resilience, and a strategic approach to wealth building. By cultivating the right habits and attitudes, you can position yourself for sustained financial growth and stability. Here's how to build a mindset for long-term financial success:

1. Adopt a Growth Mindset:
Embrace a growth mindset, characterized by a belief in the ability to learn, adapt, and grow over time. View financial challenges and setbacks as opportunities for growth and learning rather than insurmountable obstacles. Cultivate a positive attitude toward financial education, personal development, and continuous improvement.

2. Set Clear Financial Goals:

Define clear, specific, and achievable financial goals that align with your values, priorities, and aspirations. Whether it's saving for retirement, buying a home, paying off debt, or starting a business, setting goals provides direction and motivation for your financial journey. Break down large goals into smaller, actionable steps to make progress over time.

3. Practice Delayed Gratification:

Develop the habit of delayed gratification by prioritizing long-term goals over short-term pleasures. Avoid impulsive spending and instant gratification in favor of saving and investing for the future. Understand that sacrificing immediate wants for future financial security is essential for long-term wealth building and financial success.

4. Cultivate Financial Discipline:

Cultivate discipline in managing your finances by adhering to a budget, living within your means, and avoiding unnecessary debt. Develop the habit of tracking expenses, controlling impulse purchases, and prioritizing needs over wants. Practice self-control and restraint when it comes to spending and saving decisions.

5. Embrace Resilience in the Face of Challenges:
Recognize that setbacks and challenges are inevitable on the path to financial success. Develop resilience by adopting a proactive and solution-oriented mindset when faced with financial obstacles. Learn from failures, adapt to changing circumstances, and persevere in pursuit of your long-term goals.

6. Educate Yourself About Personal Finance:
Invest in your financial education by learning about personal finance concepts, principles, and strategies. Take advantage of books, articles, courses, workshops, and online resources to expand your knowledge and skills. Stay informed about economic trends, investment opportunities, and financial best practices to make informed decisions.

7. Practice Consistent Saving and Investing:
Make saving and investing a priority by consistently allocating a portion of your income toward building wealth. Automate contributions to savings accounts, retirement accounts, and investment portfolios to ensure regular and disciplined saving habits. Take advantage of compound interest and long-term investment growth to accelerate wealth accumulation over time.

8. Develop a Long-Term Perspective:
Adopt a long-term perspective on financial planning and investment decisions. Recognize that building wealth takes time, patience, and perseverance. Avoid chasing short-term gains or succumbing to market volatility by staying focused on your long-term financial goals and maintaining a diversified investment strategy.

9. Seek Opportunities for Growth and Improvement:

Continuously seek opportunities for personal and professional growth that can enhance your earning potential and financial prospects. Invest in acquiring new skills, advancing your education, and exploring entrepreneurial ventures that align with your interests and goals. Stay open-minded and adaptable to changing opportunities and market dynamics.

10. Surround Yourself with Supportive Influences:

Surround yourself with supportive influences, including mentors, peers, and role models who share your commitment to financial success. Seek guidance and advice from experienced individuals who can offer valuable insights and perspectives on wealth building and financial planning. Build a network of like-minded individuals who can provide encouragement, accountability, and support along your financial journey.

You may develop the routines, mentality, and actions required for sustained financial success by embracing these ideas and incorporating them into your everyday life. Though accumulating money is a path that calls for perseverance, commitment, and patience, you may reach your financial objectives and establish a better future for your loved ones and yourself if you have the correct mentality.

www.ingramcontent.com/pod-product-compliance
Lightning Source LLC
Chambersburg PA
CBHW050306230526
45471CB00005B/2053